Life One Breath Away

Dr Ronald Bishop

Publisher, Copyright and Additional Information

Life One Breath Away by Dr Ronald Bishop

DoctorRonaldBishop.com

Editing by Tammy Kling

Cover design by Syril Lagapa Pulido

Interior design by Rafael Andres

Contents

Acknowledgement

I would like to dedicate this book to my dear friend, the late Dr. Frank Benson, who was a brilliant Emergency Medicine Physician. He devoted his entire life to the practice of Medicine. I want to give gratitude to my mother and her twin sister Henrietta Sims and Jenette Hill for the support you have given me through out my entire life. Since your passing, I miss you both every day. To my beautiful wife Beverly Denise, thank you for our three beautiful children. Without your love and support, I would not be able to make this book possible. To my children Rhonda Ashley, you are amazing, smart, and generous. I am very proud of you and all your success. To my daughter Brittany Danielle, you are one of the most dedicated individuals I know.

You have a heart of gold and an incredible work ethic. I thank you for my three beautiful grandchildren and they are the love of my life. To my son and my fraternity brother in Kappa Alpha Psi, Brandon Corey., I am very proud of you. It was a privilege to watch you complete your dual-degree program, earning a master's degree in IT and a MBA, while working full-time and having a baby. I was so proud sitting at your graduation realizing you were the only one with a double masters is one the proudest moments of my life. Thank you for my beautiful granddaughter, Corey Leigh for she is an angel. To my grandson Julius, you are one amazing young man, and I am very proud of you.

I know you will do great things in your future. To my grandson Jayden, you are one of the most compassionate individuals I know. I see a great future for you, and I know you will do incredible things in your future.

To my granddaughter Journey, you are the most charismatic and intelligent young lady for such a young age of four. Your future is very bright, and I know that you will be famous one day. To my sister Venita, I am forever indebted for your sacrifice for caring for our mother and aunt until the day of their death. You are one the most courageous individuals I know and my love for you is ever lasting. To my brother Rodney, the love we share is incredible and having you in my life is a true blessing. I must thank our dear friend and author Andrea Collier for her encouragement and guidance through this process of writing. I want to thank her for the headshot on the cover of my book. To all my friends in the organizations that I belong, your friendship is priceless. I give all Glory to God the Almighty and am very appreciative for the opportunity to write this book. To Dee Freeman, Tammy Kling and Dr. Dale Okorodudu, thank you for inspiring me to complete this book as a part of my legacy and history.

About the Author

Dr. Ronald Bishop is a Board-Certified Emergency Medicine Physician who is a Fellow in the College of Osteopathic Emergency Physicians. A Fellow of the College is the highest honors among his colleagues. Born in the segregated South, he experienced the Fifties and Sixties culture of the Civil Rights Movement including segregation, race riots, hatred, racism and violence. He has been able to achieve his childhood dream of becoming a doctor and now wishes to encourage others. Ronald is an author, speaker, teacher, father, grandfather, and very proud husband.

Dr. Bishop decided to write about his unique experience in order to share with his readers the journey that took him from the partially segregated South to the boardrooms in the North. His experience has taught him many lessons on dealing with death, trauma and abuse as a child. In this book he writes about childhood trauma, and how he was able to overcome it to become successful despite the naysayers.

Life… One Breath Away, is about a young Black man who grew up in the South, during a time of segregation and race riots. He had a dream at the age of five years old to one day become a doctor. This unusual dream, especially from one so young, came from a conversation with his father. His father wanted to become a doctor, but life's circumstances would not allow him to do so.

The book peers through the keen eyes of the author to see the obstacles that he faced to become an accomplished doctor. He speaks of his journey from a very young age, where he unfortunately encountered child abuse and disappointment. He remembers being forced into integration in his early years where he experienced racism. In his latter college career, racism followed, and he even experienced portions of the vileness from some of his own people. Dr. Ronald

Bishop reminisces about many personal struggles with family and discloses the real difficulty of medical school. The book speaks to some health challenges as well as about some innate self-healthcare, and how he was able to manage it all. This book carries you along with him and his journey from the segregated South to the boardrooms in the North.

Introduction

What was your childhood story?

Well, may I share mine with you?

Mine began as a small Black boy growing up in the real Southern Birmingham, Alabama. Over the course of my roller-coaster journey, I've become a Board-Certified Emergency Physician, who has been practicing medicine for the last forty years. That's what I do, but let me tell you who I truly am. I am a Black man who has found his way from the segregated South to the boardrooms of the North. I have decided to take this opportunity to share my story with you. For I truly want anyone and everyone to see that you, too, can fulfill your goals and dreams. It does not matter where you were born or where you grew up or what challenges crossed your path.

Mine is a story of adversity, growth, racism, strength, and the persistence to carry on and move forward. These are the traits I hope will shine through to each one of you who have chosen to pick up this book; to peruse the pages and maybe read it from the beginning to ending.

A lot of kids go through a lot of things. In fact, youths and young adults go through a multitude of seen and unforeseen things, and my life was no different. I had many obstacles to face early on in life, beginning with being born to a young, twenty-year-old, unwed, inexperienced Black female.

We all understand the challenges single moms go through, (at least many of us do) and my mother certainly had her share of uncertainties and hardships. She had thought she'd be marrying her lover and my biological father. But the planned marriage fell completely apart, and she was stood up at the wedding ceremony. Left not only standing there at the alter alone but left with a role in life she was not prepared to take on alone.

Later, after an awful and embarrassing time, she was told that this individual had gotten someone else pregnant and had decided to marry that person instead. Feeling brokenhearted and devastated, she knew she had to find a way to raise her child as a single parent, while also struggling through college, as she tried to pursue her own education. It was at this very point in life, that my mom taught herself the real meaning of dedication.

Today's single moms have challenges, but decades ago the adversity and judgmental stigmas they faced were much greater. This was a time when it was not socially acceptable to have a child and not be married. She turned to her family for moral support to help her raise her child. They all agreed to help her with whatever support she would need. Though she felt helpless and ashamed, she decided she must continue her education. She already had a good and useful talent, as she played piano. So, she hired out to play for the school choir as that is what she really wanted to do... to become a music teacher.

Fate would raise its ugly head, and just before

graduating from college, she would be raped by a professor at the college she attended. Even though she reported this incident to the leaders and administration at the facility, no charges were ever filed against their own faculty member. She was once again faced with having the baby. Although this time, she allowed her older sister to claim ownership of the child to avoid any further embarrassment. So, the two of us young children grew up thinking we were cousins until the truth finally came out.

Did my mother's story impact my own? I feel it did and does have a real impact. Despite the hardship she must have endured throughout those years, I have great respect and love for her. I also have that same respect for anyone who persists in the face of trauma and adversity. Sometimes…many times there is no justice, yet we must continue with our lives despite injustices, prejudices and unfair circumstances. As you may or may not know…this is not an easy task to handle nor to take lightly.

As our lives continued, fate would have another chance to make life challenging. The sexual predator left the college, probably relieved of his duties, never to return. This situation left my mom in a difficult situation, where she had to fabricate who the father of this other child was. She did what she needed to do to retain her sanity and kept this a secret for many years. She allowed her older sister to remain the "mother" of the child until this older sister decided to move to Cleveland, Ohio, to live with another family member… their older brother. This action left my real sister living as my cousin in the same household. Now the mother she knew had left her and moved to a different state.

Between the shared duties of my mother, her twin sister and their older brother, they managed to take care of us both. We thrived while growing up in a loving, blended household. A few years after the oldest sister had moved away, the family learned that she had taken ill. She had been born with a hole in the middle of her heart and she now needed surgery to correct the heart problem. She ended up having the painstaking surgery, but with the complications that set in after the surgery, she passed away. Now my (cousin) sister, who is still so very young, is told that her mother has passed away. The funeral was held in Cleveland. Though young myself, I remember my sister and I were unable to travel to the funeral. At that time, I didn't ask questions, but I thought it seemed strange. Later, I found out why. For the time being, we were both left to live in the house as cousins, but my cousin began to receive a lot more attention from my mother and my aunt. Then a bit later, old truth had to come out. This untruth could no longer be perpetuated. We were of school age and entering school brought on more responsibilities.

In my role today in the Emergency Room, I see countless patients who have been subjected to various degrees of trauma, I understand that many are keeping secrets. My background has helped me see these people through the lens of empathy, while understanding that everyone's "story" is different.

What's your story?

Please turn the page and stay with me to learn more about mine.

Do not conform to the things of this world. Romans 12:2

Chapter One

Life and Death

Life is just a breath away. This is more than just a simple cliché; it's a reality that most people just can't comprehend.

Why aren't we aware of our own mortality? In our youth we believe we are invincible, and yet at some point we discover that we aren't.

Life is fragile. Most humans don't understand their mortality or the brevity with which a life can be taken. As an ER doctor for thirty-eight years, I've seen this countless times. You take one breath, and then you don't breathe anymore. There's a sense of calm over the body. The pupils dilate and become fixed, and it's almost as if that person has taken off from their body, for some destination unknown. They are here and then they're gone, and sometimes it seems as if there's no reasonable explanation.

As a healthcare professional who has been at the bedside of many dying patients, there have been times I've discovered a supernatural element at work that is far beyond my control. Working in the medical arena, in the ER, you see all kinds of crazy things. Some are simple and some are complex. There was the guy who arrived with a curling iron in his rectum, and I imme-diately called one of my surgeons to stay on backup in case I couldn't fix it. To make a long story short we had a nurse start an IV, we gave him morphine, and we sedated him. When he came to, he was all better, we removed the device, and he was eternally grateful. Because of the high dosage of medication, he had no recollection of any of what happened, and his wife picked him up and took him home.

Unfortunately, that same scenario has happened several times with different objects. Humans can do things to themselves and to one another that cause them to end up in the emergency room, and often it's especially cruel. There are suicides, injuries from ATVs or other dangerous toys that parents give their kids. Then you've got the bizarre cases like the lady who lit her cigarette in her car using a propane tank that exploded in the backseat. She suffered severe burns and did not make it; she took that last breath.

Before all of this, I had no idea what I'd face in the future, nor did I realize what was possible.

My educational journey started in Fairfield, Alabama, in a segregated community where I knew all of my neighbors and they knew me.

I attended Robinson Elementary school from first to third grade and then my life changed. I had to witness the bombing of the Sixteenth Street Baptist Church where four little girls were killed. My mother and I were three blocks away from the church when the bomb went off at another church. My grandmother was a member of the church that was bombed, and my aunt was inside the church when the bomb exploded. My grandmother was en route to the church when the bomb exploded and had to turn around and go home to be safe. Though my aunt was not physically harmed in the church, she suffered through a lot of trauma as a result.

My grandmother was the matriarch of the family and fearing for our safety decided to send my sister and me to live with her cousin, who lived in a small town. The town was called Uniontown, Alabama. It was extremely segregated, so much so, that the name written on the front of the building was… Uniontown Negro Elementary School— This was the new school we both would attend. This was also a new experience… one that I will never forget. I realized that I lived two houses from the now-actor Anthony Cox, who lives in California now and whose movies I have seen.

To get acclimated to our new surroundings and give us a well-rounded education, my cousin took us to the farms to show us how to pick cotton. We learned what a cotton gin looked like and how the farmers would take the cotton to the gin to be processed. We blended in and mixed well with the other children. Even though all the kids were poor, they all seemed happy, for poverty was simply a way of life in Uniontown for the people of color.

The real truth about my then-cousin, now my sister, had to come out when we were sent to live with my grandmother's cousin.

At the elementary school, we had all-Black teachers. My cousin Nettie was very happy to have us living with her and called us her children, for she never had the opportunity to have children of her own. She had been married to a blacksmith by the name of Christopher Smith. He died unexpectedly and she lived alone in this very large house. She was a very proper lady, who taught us right from wrong. She wanted everything to be in its proper place. She even changed my last name from Bowman to Bishop. On my birth certificate my last name was Bowman, named after my father. She did not want us going to school as brother and sister with two different last names. The problem with the name change was that she never got it changed legally.

We lived in Uniontown for two years, from the fourth through the fifth grade. I remember going to Selma with my cousin to shop, which was twenty miles from Uniontown. My cousin told us that there was a very large march in Selma with many people walking. I later learned how very close we were to the history making "March". The March from Selma to Washington DC.

After spending two years with cousin Nettie, my mother decided she wanted her children to come back home to Birmingham, Alabama. I remember going to the bus station to come home from Uniontown to Birmingham and my cousin took us to the back of the bus station to get the tickets to ride the bus. She allowed us to travel alone and told us we had to sit in the back of the bus. As a small child I could not understand why I could not sit in front of the bus when she paid for our tickets.

It wasn't much later that the Rosa Parks situation arose. I then began to realize … we as Black people were treated very differently because of the color of our skin. While living in Uniontown there were no Black doctors and I saw that my cousin had to go to the back door of the white doctor's office to get medical care. This was a critical moment in my life … I thought I should become a doctor and come back and take care of these Black people. I believe that's where the title "The Country Doctor" came from. The folk who came back to help those left behind.

We left Uniontown with sadness and regret. We had to leave our beloved cousin Nettie alone and go back to Birmingham. By this time my mother had decided to marry a man whom I had met briefly. That brief encounter let me know he really didn't like me very much, as our interactions were much different than how he would interact with or how he treated my sister. We lived in Titusville in a small, two-bedroom apartment. My sister and I had to share a room. You may or may not know about old fashion grandmothers. But this did not sit right with my grandmother, who told my mother point blank, that we were too old to be sleeping in the same room. Nothing actually changed the situation, but my mother knew how grandma felt.

We both also attended the Catholic school Our Lady of Fatima, where we had Black teachers and a white nun and a white priest. I played football and basketball to keep me active and busy... to also stay away from home.

Chapter Two

Memories

Even after you've worked hard and created success for yourself, your childhood remains a part of who you are. You can go to university or medical school and become anything you want to be, but you may still carry the pain of adversity with you. I was once that young kid growing up against all odds, and I want every kid, Black, white or Asian, to understand that they can do it, too. You can overcome.

I had the fortitude to succeed, and I was going to. But it wasn't without hurt, stress and adversity along the way.

One Sunday morning in the eighth grade my life

took a different turn. My mother had gone to church, and I had planned on going to Mass after I had something to eat. My mother's husband told me that I could not put butter on my bread for my sandwich. Now, I knew this guy didn't like me the day they got married. I wasn't even invited to the wedding. He just showed up in the picture.

I asked him why not, and he said, Because I said so.

I went to get ready for church and he began to beat me, and as I shielded myself from getting too hurt, I ran, and I was able to get away from him and went on to church.

When I returned, he told my mother I could not come back into the apartment, and he pulled out a gun.

My mother rushed me out of the apartment and took me to my grandmother's house back in Fairfield.

My grandmother then called my father and told him he had to come and get me to live with him because I couldn't live with her, and he had to step up.

I moved in with my father's mother and twin sister, his wife, and new baby brother in a three-bedroom house with one bathroom. This move changed my life significantly, for I had to travel to school catching two buses to attend school, when my mother lived two miles away from the school I attended. This meant I had to get up at 5:30 in the morning to catch a 6 a.m. bus and make a transfer downtown to get to class by 8 a.m. I stayed after school for football practice until 5:30 then caught a bus at 6 p.m. back home, arriving sometimes at 7:30 at night. This went on for several months and I had to grow up fast. One night I noticed that my stepmother and my aunt got into an argument that resulted in a physical fight, with my grandmother joining in to harm her. I intervened and hit my aunt and grandmother to keep them off my stepmother. That night my dad worked second shift and as he arrived home my mother was told to come and get me because I could no longer stay in the house.

My mother had to come and pick me up at midnight to take me back to the apartment with her husband who had pulled a gun on me and put me out. I felt so alone and abandoned at this time in my life. I decided to avoid him and concentrate on sports, playing football and basketball and running track.

This allowed me to stay away from home as much as possible to avoid conflict and being mistreated.

Life was hard but it was all I knew.

I completed the eighth grade and was then bused into integration to go to the white school. Ramsay High School at the time was eighty percent white and twenty percent Black. This was my first time integrating with a large amount of white people. I witnessed many fights in the halls and classrooms. There was a food fight in the cafeteria because the food was not up to par with the Black kids. I decided to try out for the basketball team and the coach came to me and said that I could not play because my birth certificate had a different last name on it. This is the point in my life where I had to call my dad to ask if he would allow me to make my name change permanent. My mother had to get an attorney to search vital records in Cincinnati, Ohio, to find my birth record to make my name officially Bishop. I was then able to play on the freshman team. I then noticed that there were several Black players on the varsity team who were very talented. They were playing for a state championship, and I learned a great deal from them, for they took me under their wings and taught me a lot. My freshman year I met my friend Danny Taylor, who was a year ahead of me and we bonded not knowing our mothers were good friends and had gone to school together. He is no longer with us today, for he unfortunately passed away. We went everywhere together; we shared a great friendship which help me stay away from home. I then met my first girlfriend, Robbie, and we dated for three years, and I was able to spend a lot of time with her family, but we broke up. My next girlfriend was named Vanessa, and she and I bonded, for we both aspired to become doctors. I became the captain of the basketball team and joined the Latin club and took as many science courses as possible. The rest of high school was enjoyable, for I had friends from the basketball team, and I had a girlfriend with the same goals as me. I became the president of my senior class and was voted most popular of the class.

I can remember during my senior year we lost two of my classmates, Gary and Johnny from the basketball team. Gary was murdered by a gunshot and Johnny died in a severe car accident. It was very hard for me to lose close friends at such an early age. One incident comes close to my heart: Two of my friends skipped school and went to the one friend's house. Somehow, they found a gun, which had a bullet in the chamber. My friend, joking around, pointed the gun at his friend and the bullet went off and killed my and his best friend. These were some of the most difficult times early on in my educational career. Later my friend who accidently shot the kid ended up getting arrested for trying to rob a store. He was later found dead in the jail cell and the story goes he committed suicide almost one year to the day of the accident. These were two of the worst funerals I had to attend at such a young age. The lesson I learned was that guns are dangerous, and they are not to be played with, especially if you don't know how to use them.

Graduating with a 3.4 GPA I was certain that I would attend UAB to prepare myself for their medical school. I found out that I didn't get accepted and I was devastated. My mother asked me what my plans were and I said I'd get a job. Her answer was army, to

Vietnam, or college. My answer was college, and where do I go to college? She had plans that I had no idea about. She was looking out for me.

She took me to Miles College where she got her degree and had me register. While registering I was asked what would be my major and I responded biology with a minor in chemistry because I wanted to become a doctor. She laughed, which I thought was strange, but I realized the expectations for a Black man to become a doctor were low.

Starting college, I continued to live with my mother and stepfather, but I worked in the evening in a bar washing glasses at a local hotel and I would not get off until 12 midnight.

I would come home and complete my homework and go to class the next day. After my first semester I decided to pledge a fraternity, Kappa Alpha Psi, along with ten other young men. We became bonded like no other relationship, and we continue to remain close today. We had a line name of Heaven's Eleven and we each bonded together to get through the rigorous pledging process. My second year in college gave me the opportunity to attend Fisk University for the summer for premed students. The classes were taught by the professors at Meharry Medical College. This was my first exposure to medical students who looked like me, and the professors also. The professors were authors of some of the books used in medical school. This summer program gave me inspiration that I too could be a doctor.

Returning to my third year, a tragic thing happened to my chemistry professor. He was murdered on campus shortly after my 8 a.m. class by a nonstudent. He was stabbed in the back of the neck with a screwdriver, and he died two days later. This was a week prior to midterms and our exam was supposed to be the following week. I was devastated, for he was an awesome teacher and he taught organic chemistry which I needed to apply to medical school. At the time of his death, I had a 69 GPA with 70 being passing in his class.

We didn't have class until two weeks before the end of the semester. They found a Black female to teach the class and she came in, gave one lecture and an exam the following week. Having missed over half the semester I was sure I would get one point to get a passing grade. I found out that this woman gave me a D in organic chemistry. I was outraged and went to talk to her. I told her that I could not afford to have a D on my transcript, for I wanted to apply to medical school. She replied, WHO DO YOU THINK IS GOING TO LET YOU IN MEDICAL SCHOOL? YOU ARE A PRETTY BOY AND YOU NEED TO GO AND BE A PIMP. This was not me or someone I wanted to become, and for her as a Black woman to tell me this hurt my heart. Here again, these are my own people working against me just to get my dream to come true.

Chapter Three

Overcomer

At some point in life, you reach a crossroads where you have to make a decision not to listen to the people who could crush your dreams.

The sad reality is that many people listen to the dream killers. Adversity can come from outside the family, but it can come from inside, too. Sometimes it's even teachers, friends, so-called mentors or adults who give bad advice.

Maybe they never had dreams of their own or simply gave up on them. But you can't listen. You've got to put blinders on, grab your dreams, and go after them. Sometimes you've got to distance yourself from your friends, teachers, or enemies.

I was taken aback and in disbelief that my professor, a woman of color, would tell me something of this magnitude. I went to my advisor, and she informed me there was nothing she could do. I went to the president of the college and there was nothing he could do. The registrar at the time offered to change the grade and I refused.

I then decided to join the concert choir. My cousin was the pianist, and our choir director was a very prominent and talented musician. He arranged for us to travel the entire East Coast, starting in Georgia all the way to Connecticut, down to New York and into Philadelphia. In Philadelphia, I had a strange sensation come over me when I was there. We completed the tour in two weeks, so I was excused from my chemistry class but was able to make up the work. More on the Philadelphia experience later. My cousin the pianist came to my rescue when my roommate in college moved out because he was a year ahead of me and he graduated. I could not afford to live alone in the apartment by myself and I went to him, and he agreed to move in with me and help pay the rent. The situation got very complicated, for he was gay, and I had no problem with that but after having several fights with his boyfriend things got very uncomfortable. He had bought all new furniture for the entire apartment and would not let me pay my part of the rent. We both then decided it would be best for him to be on his own because he realized that as my cousin I didn't need to be in that environment. I will never forget what he did for me, for he always looked out for me even after he left. I then had to find a new roommate and I found the roommate of a lifetime in Maurice Pompey. We got along very well, and he ended up pledging the same fraternity, Kappa Alpha Psi. Now we were roommates and brothers and lifelong friends. He later graduated and became an attorney in a small town in Alabama.

I ended up taking the class over from the same person who told me to go and become a pimp. I worked very hard to pass the class, but she made it very difficult. I then asked a young lady in the class if I could study with her because she was making all As. She agreed and I knew everything she knew but when we took the same exam, she got an A and I got a C. I then knew this person had it out for me. I continued to work hard and at the end of the class she said she would give me a C. Shortly after that semester I returned to Fisk University for the summer program and had a wonderful experience—until I had my exit interview. I was told by the admissions clerk that there would be no way that I would get into anyone's medical school with a D on my transcript. I was devastated and felt defeated, for these are people that look like me and they continued to put me down.

This was a critical point in my life. I met Dr. Frank Benson who was a Black physician who graduated from Howard University and came to Alabama to complete a Public Health Scholarship obligation in a physician-shortage area. My fraternity brothers found him and brought him to meet me. When we first met, I asked him was he a real doctor and he smiled and said yes. I replied by touching him and saying I want to be just like you.

This began a lifelong relationship until death. I got a job at ACIPCO, which is a steel plant, during the summer of my senior year. This job had me pouring hot magnesium into frames and dropping them into a barrel.

The temperature was 1,200 degrees and the first night I burned myself several times. My manager was a white man whose job was to watch me to make sure that I was able to produce so many discs per shift. When I had a lunch break, I asked him what level of education he had, and he told me he graduated from high school—barely. This was a moment that I promised myself that I would do everything in my power to become a doctor just like my friend and mentor Dr. Benson. I graduated from Miles College with a 3.4 GPA despite the adversity that I had experience from my own people. I was praying this would be enough to get me into a medical school somewhere to fulfill my dream since I was five years old.

My relationship with my high school sweetheart continued and she continued to encourage me, and I did the same for her. I remember going over to UAB for an interview with my girlfriend and we were told that we should look at becoming a respiratory therapist or something else other than a doctor. This was a Black man from the school telling us this information. We both looked at each other and said this will not stop us from becoming a doctor. She met a new doctor in town by the name of Dr. Robert Cain who had a twin brother who attended a school in Philadelphia, Philadelphia College of Osteopathic Medicine. We both had never heard of osteopathic medicine, but Dr. Cain asked us to apply. While waiting for an answer I enrolled in an anatomy class and went on to become an EMT at UAB. This required me to ride on ambulances and I had the opportunity to meet Dr. Rick Ransom, who was the medical director of the UAB emergency department. I was so elated that I too could one day be like him. I found a job at UAB on the cardiac unit and worked for a renowned open-heart surgeon by the name of Dr. John Kirkland on his post-op unit. My job was to operate the computer when patients came from the operating room to monitor their vital signs, take their blood, and give blood, albumin, nitroprusside to control blood pressure and measure chest-tube drainage. We would clean the beds and report the electrolytes. This job allowed me to see up close what the doctors and residents were doing to care for these very sick patients. Dr. Kirkland would perform a special procedure on newborn babies with tetralogy of Fallot—congenital heart deformities. I even thought that this would be an awesome thing to do.

By this time Frank and I and my fraternity brother Maurice Pompey and friend Michael Larkin had become roommates. Frank bought a large house and invited us to live with him to save money to prepare for medical school. My girlfriend and I broke up but we both applied to the same medical school. I got a letter that I got into medical school in Philadelphia, and I had no idea how I was going to live in a large city and how I was going to pay for it. Frank told me not to worry, for he had a plan, and everything would work out. My girlfriend didn't get in because I didn't get her application in on time. I felt horrible about it. Turns out she got admitted the following year.

Frank attended Wesleyan College in Connecticut and he had gone to school with several individuals who lived and worked in Philadelphia. One individual was Zane Bailey. He was the nicest guy I met on my trip for my interview for admission to medical school. Frank paid my way and had Zane to meet me at the airport and took me to his home and took me to the interview, which went well. I returned home and waited for an answer, and I was admitted to the medical school. I then thought back to the statement made by the chemistry professor and just smiled. While coming out of my interview I looked across the street from the school and I saw these satellites outside of a hotel and it occurred to me that I had been at that hotel before. When I was in the concert choir in college we sang at the same hotel. It seemed like déjà vu as I returned to Birmingham.

Now that I was accepted, I got a call from Zane informing me that I could live with him and his roommate Jesse until I could find my own place and learn my way around the city. I started school in the summer prior to the other students coming in and I met two of my lifetime friends. Wiley Sandford and Benny McKnight were both from the South like me and we bonded immediately. Wiley was repeating his first year and Benny was a science schoolteacher who was married and had three children. Wiley was in a similar situation with three kids and married to an Italian wife whom he met in Italy. More on that later, for he became my rescuer. We found ourselves in a class of 215 students with eight students of color and two were repeating from the year before.

We tried to create a group to study but quickly found that there was a lack of trust among certain individuals, and they chose to go on their own. The three of us soon became known as the Three Musketeers and we went everywhere together, and we studied together, for Wiley knew the information that was taught the year before, so we had some advantage. We quickly noticed that certain people in the school started staring at us and we had a professor approach us and ask us if we were going to try to take over the school. We felt this was rather racist.

I met several Black doctors at the school and one doctor told me the story of the conversation that occurred prior to me getting an interview.

He told me that the discussion centered around my

professor getting killed on campus and the D on my transcript. He then informed me that the president of the college, Dr. Thomas Rowland, entered the meeting and asked the question did I kill the professor and the answer was no.

He then instructed them to give me an interview. Dr. Rowland and I became friends after I got admitted to the school.

Chapter Four

Supernatural

There's no doubt that there's a higher power, when you can observe the miracles that occur in the ER. I've delivered babies in the elevator before, and I've watched young people pass on before their time. It often comes full circle. My life has been enriched by the process, and if this kid with a dysfunctional family can do it, so can you, or anyone. We just must be able to overcome our psychological pain and challenges. The negative words from adults and the abuse I faced at the hands of my stepfather were a springboard that launched me to my success! I turned a corner and I thought: I will prove you wrong.

And I did!

What you'll find along the way is that you begin to thrive from the achievement.

Some people become something because they have something to prove, but when they go back to visit family, nothing changes. You can't earn the respect of people who are committed to hate or bitterness for no reason. You must understand that you'll face that your entire life. If you're successful, people are going to hate it.

I began to think that God had a hand in my dream to become a doctor since the age of five. One doctor, Dr. Leonard Johnson, was a graduate of the college, and he had a large family practice on Spruce Street in Philadelphia. It turns out he was my fraternity brother in Kappa Alpha Psi.

He took me under his wings and allowed me to shadow him in his office and took me on rounds to see his patients in the hospital.

He later introduced me to other Kappa brothers who were doctors in the city, and this opened many opportunities for me to learn the art of medicine.

After living with Zane, I found it difficult to study at home, so I met a female friend of his and Frank's who also attended Wesleyan and she had her own home and lived by herself. We began to date, and she invited me to move into her home with her so I could have more time to study. I agreed and we began to live together. Things were going well until I made the mistake of asking her to marry me and she said yes. We traveled to the West Coast to meet her family and they were excited that she was going to marry a doctor for she had an uncle who was a doctor in California who was very successful. We then decided to travel to Alabama to meet my family and things didn't go well at all. My grandmother told me that this was not the woman for me, for she loved me becoming a doctor more that she loved me for who I was.

She then told me to inform her that I wanted to think about us getting married, being this was the first year of medical school. She also informed me to have a plan in place to have somewhere to live because she was going to put me out of her home. She was so right, and I had made plans to live with my classmate

Wiley and his three kids until I could find me a place on my own. I then called off the wedding and the relationship ended with us not being able to remain friends. I was able to find an apartment but was unable to pay the rent by myself, so I found a roommate who was in school but quickly learned that he had a substance-abuse problem. I had to part ways with him, and he was expelled from school. I then had another roommate who wasn't in school, and we didn't see eye to eye when it came time for me to study. I continued to do well in school, for I was studying with my two friends in the library at the college.

While shadowing Dr. Johnson I met a very nice young lady who was a nurse and we dated for a brief period, but I was not able to be serious in a relationship after the breakup and cancelled wedding. I completed my first year of medical school and stayed for the summer and did research in the physiology lab on cutting-edge experiments on hypokalemic cardiac arrest during open-heart surgery. We would do the work on the heart of a dog and measure the enzymes in the heart after it has been stopped and how long it would take to get the heart restarted. This research was important for the open-heart procedures done on humans during bypass surgery. This became very interesting for I had worked in a unit back home that performed open-heart surgery and was able to care for the patients after returning from surgery. This sparked my interest in becoming a heart surgeon.

The research got published and had my name in the paper. This made me very proud and gave me inspiration to continue my goals to complete medical school education.

Prior to my second year I walked across the street from the school to go to the bank and as I was walking, I saw this young lady walking into the bank, so I followed her in but got cold feet to say anything to her. I went to the teller and asked for my balance and while standing there I saw this beautiful small-framed young lady who had a gorgeous smile and high heels with long beautiful hair. She smiled and she was very friendly but had on what I thought was a wedding ring. I said to her you are awfully friendly to be married. She then informed me that she wore the ring to keep the men from hitting on her. I asked her how I could get in touch with her and she wrote her number on the back of my receipt and said DON'T WAIT TOO LONG TO USE IT. I was so excited I went back and told my friends that I had met this beautiful woman and I could not wait to ask her out. I waited a few days and called to set up a date for lunch.

When I showed up at the bank for lunch another man came into the bank stating he would like to take her to lunch also. She politely told him he was not invited, and she was going to lunch with me. This was the beginning of a very long relationship. At lunch we talked about what we liked about each other and what we wanted the next five years. After lunch I raced back to school to tell my friends about the exciting young lady I had met at the bank. They named her the Banker. We continued to communicate but I had to get some of my affairs under control. On my birthday, one of the individuals came to my apartment unannounced and this caused the Banker to break up with me. I then set the record straight and told the other individual that I needed to go in a different direction and pursue my heart, which was with the Banker. I went to her home and met her mother, and it was love at first sight. She was this sweet-hearted woman, and I knew she had raised a beautiful young lady. I took my friend Benny, and he played the piano while I asked for her to forgive me and told her I would make things right. She agreed and we dated for the rest of my medical school career. I met the rest of her family and found out that she lost her father at the age of twelve, for he died in her arms of a massive stroke. She was raised by her mother who suffered much grief from the loss of her husband, whom she was totally dependent on. She had to grow up fast to help her mother overcome the depression and her mom had to find work while she attended school.

My third and fourth years in medical school went well, for I had to travel to different hospitals to do my rotations. During my fourth year I decided to take the Banker to meet my family in Alabama. My mother fell in love with her, but my grandmother still had her reservations. We got engaged on Valentine's Day and my graduation was coming up in June.

My mother suggested that since I was graduating, we should get married the week after graduation since the family had planned to attend the graduation. The Banker thought this was a great idea and we returned to Philadelphia to plan a wedding. We were able to put it all together and all my friends from college and some from high school were a part of the ceremony. My entire family attended the graduation and the wedding, except my stepfather, who would not attend the wedding but was at the graduation.

This was the same person who told me I would not be anything. We had a total of twenty-six people in the wedding party and had a sit-down dinner and open bar for the reception. My friend Frank was my best man, and my sister and niece were in the wedding party. My mother was a wedding planner and she insisted that we have a second reception in Birmingham for her friends a week after our wedding in Philadelphia. So, the Banker became Mrs. Beverly Denise Bishop, and we were so happy and in love. All my friends loved her, and they were happy for me, for I had found my life partner. The reception in Birmingham was done very well. We had a harpist, food and a lot of her friends and relatives who could not make the wedding in Philadelphia. We returned to Philadelphia for me to start my rotating internship.

I began to like a small hospital in Langhorne, Pennsylvania, by the name of Delaware Valley Medical Center. I was able to match with the hospital to do my rotating internship. I was the only African American in the class, but we were very close. My internship went well, and I started looking at what type of residency I wanted to follow. It turns out that the hospital built a new facility which I had the opportunity to be a part of. We had to find a way to discharge all the patients and move into the new facility. Towards the end of my internship the hospital got a new residency program in emergency medicine and there were two positions available, which I interviewed for, along with my colleague and friend Dr. Michael Farmer. I also interviewed for the surgical program and was told there were concerns that I would be discriminated against for being African American and an osteopathic doctor. This was told to me by a general surgeon who truly had my best interest at heart, and I appreciated the advice. The surgeon was from a Jewish background, and he understood being discriminated against from his personal experience. I decided to go into emergency medicine, which was the same as my best man, Dr. Frank Benson. He was so proud of me when I called and told him the news.

During the first year of my residency and being married I didn't have a lot of time to spend at home, for the program required twelve-hour shifts seven days a week with one day off and then working night shift, seven at night to seven in the morning. My wife and I made the best of the time we had together, and we found out that she was pregnant with our first child. We were very excited but soon found out that she had a miscarriage. This was very devastating and created doubt in her mind if she would be able to have children, which we both wanted.

I continued to work hard in my program and met some awesome physicians who mentored me and taught me very well. One of them, Dr. Stephan Kosmorsky, became one of my best friends and the godfather of my second daughter. I mention him because we were involved in a severe car accident while I was driving his car and fell asleep, hitting a post and totaling the car, and he had severe, life-threatening injuries. I felt horrified and my wife was eight and a half months pregnant with our first child when this happened. I remember she had to get a ride to come to the emergency room to see me because she wasn't able to drive. It took me a long time to get over the emotional repercussions of what happened, and I was able to visit my friend on a frequent basis to make sure he would recover from his severe injuries. He never blamed me for what happened, and we remain close friends even today.

Our first child was born on July 31st, and we were very happy to receive a beautiful daughter. We named her Rhonda Ashley, and my wife was an awesome mom. Two days after coming home with the baby I got a call from her mom that my wife was having trouble breathing and needed me to come home right away. When I got home, she was having severe difficulty breathing so I rushed her to the hospital where

I worked. Upon arrival my colleagues took over and gave her excellent care. We soon found out that she had a severe allergic reaction to the medication to dry up her breast milk. She had to stay in the ICU overnight to make sure she would be okay. She was devastated to be separated from her newborn child. We were able to get her back home pretty fast.

I was able to continue into my second year of the residency and had to travel to multiple hospitals for my training. One of my most memorable rotations was at children's hospital in Philadelphia. Each day we would see over one hundred children with all kinds of illnesses. One child had been put in a tub of hot water and burned both his feet and we found out it was done by his father. A ten-month-old baby boy was left on the front porch of someone's home. This rotation opened my eyes to the magnitude of child abuse and what children must go through, which is totally out of their control. I was able to understand how fortunate I was to survive some of the trauma I had experienced in my childhood. My next rotation was at a trauma center located in Allentown, Pennsylvania, where on my first day I experienced the death of a nineteen-year-old male involved in a one-car accident where he rolled a convertible on top of him and was pronounced dead in the emergency room. I experienced several cases that were very emotional.

Three of the most heartbreaking included the case of an eight-year-old boy who was skiing with his brother and hit a tree, had a closed-head injury and never woke up. Seeing him being pronounced and the family's response was heartbreaking. A thirty-seven-year-old female went out to get ingredients for her Thanksgiving dinner and was broadsided by another vehicle. She had severe injuries, and they were unable to save her. To see her young children and husband having to see her body was emotional. My next case was a sixteen-year-old male who had just dropped his girlfriend from church, ran off the road and hit a tree. He had a closed-head injury and was taken to surgery at midnight to remove blood from his brain. I remember staying up all night at his bedside to make sure he would not die. He was able to recover but had stroke-type deficits and we got him well enough to go to rehabilitation.

Those experiences help me to be able to cope with death and dying and help me understand that bad things happen to good people. I returned home and gave my wife and daughter a big hug and realized how blessed I was to have my family. Now I was near the end of my residency and had to find a place to fulfill an obligation to the Public Health Service Corps, which gave me a scholarship while in medical school. I needed to pay back three years in a physician-shortage area.

I looked at several sites and they were full, so I found a position in the state of Louisiana.

I had to travel to New Orleans to meet with the medical board, who were all white, to make sure I was able to come and practice medicine in the state, for it qualified as a physician-shortage area with the federal government. I was told that it would not be a problem, so I went back to Langhorne and told my wife that we were going to move to Hammond, Louisiana, for it was close to the hospital in Independence, a small town in Tangipahoa Parish.

Prior to us leaving we found out that we were expecting our second child, and it's a girl. We were both excited, but both of us had a huge challenge ahead of us, for we had to find somewhere to live that was safe and we only had one vehicle. We were blessed to find a gentleman who had built new condominiums in Hammond, and we were able to put down a small down payment to own it. I started working at this small hospital with twenty beds and a small emergency department. The waiting room sat over fifty to eighty patients but the emergency rooms we had to see patients in totaled only eight. The daily volume was 125 patients in a twenty-four-hour day. There was only one doctor to see the patients, for this was a charity hospital, so patients didn't have to pay for their care. People would come in pickup trucks and bring food because the wait time was six to eight hours, and I was working alone on twelve-hour shifts. This was very difficult for I had little or no time to eat or go to the bathroom. I had a great staff, who were used to this kind of volume, and we did the best we could do to care for those in poverty. I quickly learned that the state had a two-tiered health system when my wife and I found a gynecologist for our unborn child. We were instructed to go to the hospital in Hammond, for we had insurance. I would get transfers from the hospitals for patients who didn't have insurance. Where I trained in Pennsylvania this was illegal. I was told by a doctor that this was Louisiana, and this was acceptable practice. I felt horrible but proud to be able to care for them for they had nowhere else to go for their care.

Our second child was born in Hammond, and we named her Brittany Danielle. My mother-in-law traveled from Philadelphia to help us to care for the babies, for I was still working the twelve-hour shifts and was very tired all the time. After about a year and six months into my obligation I received a letter in the mail from the medical board that I could no longer practice medicine in the state of Louisiana.

This was the same board that told me that they were happy to have me come and serve in a physician-shortage area. I learned that they decided that they would not accept my board scores from Pennsylvania, and I needed to take a foreign medical graduate exam. I had completed a full rotating internship and a two-year emergency medicine residency, and this was not good enough to practice medicine. I decided to take the exam, which was two days, eight hours the first day and six hours the second. I got my scores back and it stated that I didn't pass by one point. Sounds familiar to my days back in college. I called the Public Health Service Corps and was told to take the exam again and I refused. I felt very confident that I knew the information on the exam. I decided to get a lawyer and he told me there was nothing I could do, for the board had the final decision. I asked him would this have something to do with the fact that I was an osteopathic doctor and Black. He would not answer me but the look on his face told the story. I then call the Public Health Service Corps and told them that I was going to rob a bank and tell them that I worked for them, and I was unable to make a living to take care of my family. They then told me that they would grant me a federal license, which superseded the states, and I could continue to work but I would have to take a forty-thousand-dollar pay cut and work the same hours. I met a friend who had connections to someone on the medical board and they agreed to meet with me in New Orleans. I never saw this person's face, but the message was to get out of Louisiana as soon as possible, for I would never pass any exam. After this meeting I requested a change in my site to pay back my obligation. They then responded that they had an open position in Roswell, New Mexico, and I could transfer to that location. Now I had bought a condo and made friends in the community, joined a church, and made an impression in the community.

We decided to leave the state and we accepted the position in Roswell. I remember the first flight to the town, we had to fly through Albuquerque, and we had to board this six-passenger plane where we could see the pilots flying the plane. As we were landing the plane it was swinging from side to side as it landed. We were very afraid for our lives but after we arrived, we were taken to the hospital where I would be working. The ride from the airport to the hospital we saw nothing but flat, dry land as far as we could see. We walked into the hospital and the doctor said he wanted to talk to my wife first, for if she was not happy then we would not stay. He indicated that Roswell was a small town, but they would work hard to find us a nice house and make us as comfortable as possible. We had a realtor show us several houses and we found a house that was unoccupied, and we were able to purchase the house. Now we had to fly back on the same small plane and prepare our family to move to Roswell. We had heard rumors about the aliens in the town, but we didn't take it seriously. The trip from Hammond was difficult for we had to leave the friends we had made, and although the movers came to pick up our furniture, they could not give us a date of its arrival. We took several days to travel across the entire state of Texas, and it was so hot the pavement was melting as we drove on the roads. We made frequent stops, for the kids were very small and we wanted to take our time because we didn't know how long it would take to get our furniture delivered.

We finally got our furniture and got settled and I had no problems with my license in New Mexico, for they had an osteopathic board. I started working the twelve-hour shifts, which sometimes would become twenty-four-hour shifts because of the shortage of doctors in the area. My boss at the time would work a forty-eight-hour shift and I refused to do that because I realized how dangerous this could be for the patients and for me and my health and my license.

The staff was amazing and well-trained, and we bonded and cared for the patients very well. There was a large Indian population and a large Mexican population with a very small Black population. I quickly found out that Roswell was a traffic thruway for cocaine coming from Mexico. Every day a car would pull up to the entrance of the emergency room and a person would be pushed out barely breathing from an overdose of some type of cocaine laced with some type of drug, or the strength was cut too heavy. We would rush them in and intubate them and give them Narcan and they would wake up and pull the tube out and be angry with us for ruining their high. Never mind they were a few seconds away from death. This became a normal practice during my time in Roswell.

We were able to get my oldest daughter in a preschool and my wife came home one day and said she was enrolled in school at the college in Roswell. I asked what she was going to do, and she told me she was going into the nursing program, which was for women who were stay-at-home mothers, and they had a daycare for our middle daughter. This was the perfect situation, for both children were cared for and she could go to school with my daughter and be able to check in on her during the day. She did extremely well in school, for she was a natural. She came to me in the emergency room crying and I asked her what was wrong, and she told me she was pregnant, and I told her it was going to be okay. She continued school and had a baby boy and we named him Brandon Corey.

I can remember several situations while working in the emergency department. I had worked a thirty-six-hour shift and it was around seven o'clock in the evening when a person came running through the emergency room doors saying that his friend had been injured. Turns out his friend worked at the hospital in the radiology department. They brought him in by private vehicle and could not find the entrance to the department. His friend was not breathing, and he had blood all over his face. We tried everything to revive him but were unsuccessful. We found out he was riding on the back of a pickup truck and fell headfirst onto the pavement. He had a large gash in his skull and had sustained severe brain injury.

It was not until I had pronounced him deceased that we figured out who he was and that he had been at work earlier that day. We all cried and had to call his family to let them know of his death. I had a police officer come into the emergency room and tell me he had something wrong with his rectum. I did an exam on him and found he had a mass in his rectum which turn out to be cancer. We became friends and found out the cancer had spread to the rest of his body. He began to get chemotherapy, which wasn't working so he decided to go to Mexico and try a drug not available in the United States called Laetrile. I got a call that he was coming from Mexico, near death, and they needed to fly him home so he could pass in the U.S. He passed away as soon as they landed. I was very sad to lose a friend and watch his decline so rapid. I learned how precious life can be and we are only here on this earth for short time.

My most interesting cases were individuals who had come in with certain objects in their rectum. One came in with a cucumber. He had to go to surgery to get it removed. The other presented with a vibrator, which was still running. I was able to remove that and they were very happy and embarrassed but we treated them with dignity and respect.

One of the most challenging days at work I had a gunshot wound to the chest come in and at the same time the nurse came to me and told me that my wife was in the emergency room with a severe headache a few days after having our son. The gunshot victim didn't make it and I had to speak to the family, and they were very upset. Turns out this was a domestic abuse situation, and the victim was shot by his significant other. Shortly after speaking with the family my nurse told me that my wife was going to the CAT scan for a scan of her head. I rushed to be with her, and her blood pressure was extremely high with a severe headache. The CAT scan came back positive for a small bleed in her brain. This was one of the scariest days of my life to think I could lose my wife and I thought about the kids at home with my mother-in-law. I got on the phone and called our neurosurgeon and told him what was happening, and he came over right away to take over care of my wife. He assured me she would be okay, and the bleeding had stopped, and he needed to get her blood pressure down and admit her to the hospital.

She got admitted to the ICU and while in the unit she met a Black pastor who had a church in Roswell, and he prayed for my wife. Turns out he was from Michigan and had family in Michigan. This turns out to be significant in the future, for we didn't know where we were going to end up at the time of their interaction. They were able to get her blood pressure down and she had little or no deficits as a result of the stroke. She was able to return home to our newborn child and she only had one month to finish her nursing degree. We went to see the neurosurgeon for follow up and he suggested that she not return to school, for it may be too stressful and he wanted to make sure her blood pressure would remain stable.

This was very close to the end of my obligation to

the Public Health Service Corps, and I needed to start to find a place to work because I knew we were not going to stay in Roswell.

While in Roswell I got a call from my grandmother telling me she had been having chest pain. She told me she was having difficulty breathing, so I told her to call her cardiologist. She got admitted to the hospital and we travelled to Birmingham with our two children at the time and saw my grandmother in the hospital. The doctor recommended a heart catheterization to look for blockages. She asked me what I thought, and I said I think you should go ahead and get it done. Prior to the procedure she told my wife that my wife was going to have a boy. Not knowing my wife was pregnant, we had no idea that she would know what was ahead of us at this time. I ended up regretting my advice to grandma after the procedure because shortly afterward she went into cardiac arrest and passed away. I felt horrible for I made the decision and it cost her life. We had the funeral at the Sixteenth Street Baptist Church in Birmingham, the same church that had been bombed and the three girls were killed. I had flashbacks while sitting in the church, of the stained-glass windows when I was a little boy and went to church with my mother and grandmother. She was a pianist in the church and served on many organizations and was known as the oldest member in the church at the time of her death. We returned to Roswell, and it was time for us to find a place to move.

I got a call from a very good friend of mine who I did my residency with, and he informed me that he had moved to Michigan, and he was working in the city of Detroit, Michigan. I told him that I was looking for a job and he told me he may be able to help.

Several weeks later he called and said he wanted me to come to Michigan for a job opportunity for he had some colleagues that had gotten a new contract in the City of Flint, Michigan. My wife decided to hold off on returning to school and I told her I would travel to Michigan to see if the possible job would work for me and our family. When I arrived in Detroit my friend picked me up and we traveled to Lansing, Michigan, to an attorney's office. I walked into the office to meet four other doctors and they welcomed me, and a meeting started, and a contract was prepared with my name on it. I didn't have to interview because the other doctors trusted my friend's recommendation for me work with them. I then called my wife and told her I thought this would be a good situation to get us out of Roswell and we could have a fresh start. She agreed and this was a new beginning for us to explore. I asked her if she wanted to stay and finish school and she said she wanted to be home with our newborn child and the girls.

We decided to put our house on the market to sell. We didn't have anywhere to move to but we knew we were going to leave Roswell. We put our house up on the market on Friday and it sold on Sunday. There was a person interested in buying the house due to a domestic situation.

Now we had some pressure to find a home in Michigan as soon as possible. My mother-in-law came to stay with the kids, and we traveled to Michigan. When we arrived, they had a realtor and a banker lined up for us once we picked out the right house. My wife had done some research on the Michigan school systems and the town I was to be working in was not an option for us to live. We saw several homes in the Okemos and East Lansing area and they were very expensive, and I knew I didn't have a lot of money to put a sizeable down payment on a home. We walked into this house that was empty and it had no air conditioner, and we were told you didn't need that in Michigan. Turns out they were wrong because in the summer it gets very humid and hot.

The house next door was available, and it was empty, and when we walked in my wife said, I want this house. I looked at her and thought, how are we going to be able to pay for this house? We don't have any money to afford this house. This is where God intervened on our behalf, and we met a man who became one of my best friends. The realtor set us up with a bank in Owosso, Michigan, by the name of Key State Bank. We walked into the bank and met the then-vice-president of the bank, his name was Jack Harrison, and he was the most warm, kind and caring man we met. My wife looked at him and said, I want that house, and he said, we can make that happen. I was shocked and he said he could have all the paperwork ready for us to sign and they would make the down payment reasonable for us in our situation. I could not believe what I was hearing but he was true to his word. More to come on my friend Mr. Harrison.

We traveled back to Roswell to plan to make the move to Michigan. My children were young enough that they didn't mind moving, for they had not established any significant relationships to keep us there. We made it fun, contacted a moving company, and they came and gave us a price to move our furniture; however, we had no idea that they had the ability to change the approximated weight when the truck is loaded.

So, the price that was quoted changed drastically and we were held hostage to the increase in the cost. I had bought a used car from my neighbor in Roswell and needed to sell it and it turned out he wanted to buy it back. Now that our furniture was packed up it was time to say our goodbye and the staff at the hospital gave us a party and showed us a lot of love and appreciation for the care and service to the patients that I took care of during my time there.

Life is always a series of ups and downs, curveballs and surprises, and moments of joy.

The travel to Michigan was very long, for we had three small children and one car and everything we needed for our four-month-old son. His milk, the sheets, bathtub and clothes for us and the girls. It took us four long days to make the trip. I remember being in Oklahoma and stopping at a restaurant and a storm came through and the lights went out in the restaurant before we could get our meal. We sat in the dark until the storm passed and made it back to the hotel. It was a scary moment, but the adventure had clearly begun!

We spent the night, and the storm passed the next day and we continued on our new journey to Michigan.

We arrived in Michigan and the house was ready to move into and our furniture was delayed so we had to stay in a local hotel until our furniture arrived. My mother-in-law came to be with us and the kids until we could unpack the kitchen and set up the bedrooms.

We wanted to keep them safe from all the boxes and all the disarray and chaos in the new house. A lot of married couples aren't lucky enough to have family around, but we were, and we were grateful for that. It made the entire process much easier.

It took several days for us to get the house set up the way my wife wanted. I began to work in Flint at a large hospital with a very busy emergency department. I had to drive an hour to get to work and I worked twelve-hour shifts and stayed over sometimes one to two hours doing charts. This turned out to be thirteen- to fourteen-hour days and I would have to come back the next day and do it over again.

This went on for several months and I decided that this was not a good situation for me to be in long-term. Turns out we got a new contract at a smaller hospital which was closer to our home and my drive was a half hour less time.

The emergency room was a small one and had a much smaller volume. I remember my first visit to the hospital the CEO came down and welcomed me and I felt a sense of calm that this might be a better fit for me in the long run.

Starting the new job was exciting, for we had an

amazing staff of nurses and techs with a lot of experience, and they were all from the local community.

I can still remember one of the first cases that got my attention while working the night shift. We had a male patient brought in with a gunshot wound to his head. The family stated that he was sitting in the kitchen at the table with his sister and brother, got up went into the bedroom and came back with a gun and pulled the trigger—shooting himself through the mouth and into his head.

He was still alive when he got to the hospital but not awake. I quickly intubated him and decided to transfer him to a larger hospital. The family was devastated, and I did my best to comfort them but realized that I had to care for the other patients in the department.

My experience with several patients taught me a valuable lesson on the value of life and how precious it can be. Not everyone survives, but you have to somehow find a way to help them all. It's an adrenaline rush when you do, and it's sad when life is lost.

Another very memorable patient was one who arrived to the emergency room stating that he had chest pain while watching the television show ER on TV.

He was in his thirties.

We brought him into a room and put him on a monitor and I noticed some changes on the monitor and we got an EKG and he was having a massive heart attack. We quickly started the protocol for treatment and before we could get everything going, he said, I don't feel too good. He then lost consciousness and went into a lethal rhythm. And that's how fragile life can be. This young man went from perfectly healthy to heart attack in moments.

I shocked him immediately and he woke up and looked at me and said, What happened?

I told him that his heart had stopped, and he went unconscious again. It was the strangest thing, as if angels were calling him to some unknown party or destination.

His wife was sitting in the corner watching this happen the entire time. I continued to shock his heart and give medications, but his heart would not respond. I ended up pronouncing him dead with his wife in the room. I felt terrible for I knew I did everything possible to keep him alive. But there are times when your best just isn't good enough and then you have to live with the mystery of the unknown.

His wife told me she knew that I had done every-thing, and she had a chance to see for herself the efforts we put forward to keep him with us. I then went into the back, and I cried my eyes out because I felt like it was my fault.

My staff gathered and we all cried together know-ing that we all did the right thing.

Those are the moments that bond you together forever, as crisis workers. Even your spouse would never be able to understand what you have just been through, no matter how much you explained it. There's nothing to describe the loss of life in your own hands and the weight and pressure that that places on you.

If you're a healthcare worker, EMT, or first re-sponder, you know exactly what I'm talking about. If you're not, go hug one today.

The next situation that comes to mind as a very vivid memory in the ER was that of a fifteen-year-old male who was brought into the emergency room unresponsive with no pulse. He had no signs of trauma on his body and the story goes that he came home from school and his parents went out to the store and while they were gone, he went into the garage and turned on the car with the garage door down. No one knows why, or what he was going through, but they just know that he was troubled.

He was found by the parents and EMS was called. He was dead by the time he got to me, but I had to try to do everything I could think of to get him back, but our efforts failed. The mother stood at the bedside asking him to wake up and I knew it would not happen.

My heart was broken, because he was so young and now gone and no one would ever know why he made that decision on that day.

Sometimes you have to live without answers. And this is the biggest trauma of life. It is almost impossible to live without answers. It is so difficult to live without answers. We are human and we are wired to seek answers. We were given a brain and a heart and a mind by God for that very purpose. But we were also given wisdom to understand that sometimes there are no answers. And in those moments, we just have to have faith. It may be awful, and it may be traumatic, and it may change our world forever, but we have to simply have faith that God is in control.

Someone once asked me if I had any supernatural experiences during my time in the emergency room and I said yes. There have been unexplainable moments when people died when they shouldn't have, and it seemed as if Heaven was calling them. I cannot explain this. Their lives were used to better the lives of others and they did in fact leave a legacy.

The day that a ten-month-old was brought into the emergency room unresponsive in cardiac arrest comes to mind.

We worked on this baby for what seemed like forever, and we finally got a heartbeat back. We had to transfer the baby to a larger facility, but I knew in my heart that this child would have a very slim chance of making it. It turned out that the mom had placed the child down and went to the bathroom and came back and found the child unresponsive.

The grandmother worked in the hospital, and we

are still very close today. The baby died two days later, and this was so devastating for me.

I share these tragedies with you, for most individuals would not be able to function having all this type of sorrow on a constant basis. After my shifts would be over, I would go home and hug my family and tell them how much I love them and how I appreciated my wife and how she stayed home to care for the kids in this new environment.

I continued to work the night shift and took my son to preschool in the morning. I would come home and sleep for a few hours and go back and pick him up. My wife made the decision to go back to school to complete her nursing degree, which she was unable to complete while in Roswell. She was given the option to return to Roswell or start in her second year at the local community college.

This is the reality of having a family. Life goes on whether you lose patience or not. Life goes on whether you're consumed with sorrow, or not.

After having an interview at the local community college, she came home and told me how she decided to start from the beginning. I said, WHAT?

And she told me she wasn't sure of herself, and she needed to know that she could remember the information because it was too important for her not to know. I was very supportive of her decision, but it just meant that I needed to help with the kids more.

How would an ER doctor do this? I had no idea.

Prior to starting school, she developed a heel spur on her foot, and it caused her severe pain. We went to see a foot doctor and he recommended foot surgery to remove the heel spur, thinking that she could have the surgery in August and be ready for school in September.

Well, after surgery, post-op complications came into play and the foot would not heal. She started classes on crutches, and it was very difficult to carry her books and get around to the different classes. This went on until February and we had to decide that she would withdraw and let her foot heal. We went to the dean of the college, and she agreed to save her a spot in the next class.

We finally got the foot to heal, and she returned to

school and finished with honors. During her graduation our oldest daughter got to pin her.

This was a very proud moment for me and her mother.

Our children were able to see their mom go to school and study, and I felt that helped them understand the importance of getting an education.

Most importantly, it gave them a feeling of empowerment to understand that you can accomplish anything you want to do at any age.

I continued to work on the night shift, and I got to know every state cop and sheriff deputy in the entire county.

We became friends and would hang out together after work and talk about some of the patients they would bring into the Emergency Room to me in the middle of the night.

There were occasions when I would have to care for them when they got injured on duty. This became a close-knit family, and they would not let anything happen to me. I had a situation where an angry patient was upset because she didn't get the pain medication she wanted and when I went into the room to explain why she didn't need the medication she took a cup of water and threw it in my face and called me the N-word.

Before I knew it the staff had called the police and they came and arrested her for assault. They would not tolerate anyone mistreating me while I was working.

I remember getting a call to the OB department to care for a patient in labor because her doctor had not come in time to deliver the baby. I was so nervous because it had been many years since I had delivered a baby. I remained calm and the nurses were awesome; we delivered a beautiful baby boy and mother, and baby did fine.

As soon as I had the cord cut her doctor came in and said congratulations. Turns out the mother was the wife of one of the police officers! What an amazing full-circle moment it was. I mention this story because coming home from work one morning I had a head-on collision with the same person—the woman whose child I had delivered. We both had non-life-threatening injuries, but it was very difficult for me because I was the cause of the accident, and I was talking to my wife on the phone to let her know I was on the way when the crash happened.

The officer was at the scene and came over to my car to make sure I was okay. We developed a bond, and we were grateful no one was killed. Both cars were totaled but we both survived and were able to return to work. What an awful moment. It showed me firsthand how accidents can happen even to the best of us when we aren't paying attention.

I continued to work the night shift and care for our children during the day with little sleep.

We soon learned that the administration was not happy with one of our partners and wanted to make a change in the contract. The partners met and decided to leave the hospital and let one partner run the emergency department on his own. Turns out it was an epic failure and he decided to sell the contract to the partners that left.

I then went to my friend Mr. Harrison at the bank, and he said we can make it happen. We ended up starting a whole new group and named it Tri-County Emergency Physicians. We were able to hire new physicians and provided excellent care to the local community. During that time, I began to receive several awards, among them the Liberty Bell Award from the local bar association for my willingness to testify on the cases that would come through the emergency department that required a doctor's opinion.

I would never charge for my services, for I always felt this was my way of giving back to the community. I was selected to receive the Margaret S. Gulick Humanitarian Award for community service. I would go out into the community and give lectures on asthma and COPD (chronic obstructive pulmonary disease) to the elderly population.

I decided to start the Advanced Cardiac Life Support Course in our hospital so that the staff would have the ability to be proficient in the cardiac arrest situations. The physicians could take the course for free.

The funds were provided by the medical staff, and I had full support to make the program one of the best in the area. I adopted a philosophy to teach without pressure and the students could learn with enthusiasm. I soon learned that I was chosen by my colleagues for Physician of the Year. This was a very high honor, for they recognized the care I provided to our patients and the concern I would always have for my colleagues!

But life was crazy during this season, and something had to give.

I started getting burned out working the night shift. I met this doctor at a golf outing by the name of Jack Clarkson who was a family-practice doctor in the small town of Ovid, Michigan. He offered me the opportunity to work on Fridays in his office with his wife who is a doctor, because they both played in a band.

Imagine that. He just wanted more time to explore his true passion!

They would play on the weekends, and they needed Friday to prepare for the performances. I started working and I fell in love with it and with the people in the town. Before I knew it, I was working two days a week and I was very busy.

I speak about this experience because of one case

that touched me for the rest of my life. The patient complained of what we thought was a sinus infection and I treated it with an antibiotic, yet several weeks later there was no improvement.

I changed to a stronger antibiotic and waited a few more weeks and still no improvement. I then decided to order a CAT scan and there was a large tumor in the sinus cavity. The tumor was malignant, and several consultations recommended surgery.

The surgery was very extensive; the tumor was removed and the bone in the face was replaced with a bone from the arm. The treatment was successful and one evening several years after he was cancer-free, I see a wife and a baby boy walking down the street. I cried, for I knew that God had intervened on his behalf and saved his life. There was a second child, and he is still cancer-free today. This experience taught me again how precious life can be.

Sometimes God lets you see the role that you have played.

I started teaching at Michigan State College of Osteopathic Medicine after I was asked by Dr. Margaret Aguwa, a prominent physician in the college. She wanted to have more presence of physicians of color in the college for the students. I was reluctant in the beginning, for I had never thought about teaching.

But I started and fell in love with it and soon knew that this was my opportunity to give back with my knowledge and experience. What an amazing season and revelation! When you know you've found your purpose, it is invigorating and exhilarating.

One day before class I experienced the worst pain I had in my life. I suddenly heard a loud sound in my lower back to the point I was unable to walk. My son was home at the time, and he called 911. I ended up in the emergency room with a severely herniated disc in my lumbar spine. I was not able to work for several weeks. It was devastating.

I had physical therapy and injections in my back, but nothing seemed to help. It was decided that I needed surgery to remove the disc off my nerve. Prior to the surgery I developed some chest pain when I would take a deep breath. I tried to ignore it, but it became very severe. My wife looked at me and said, You have a blood clot in your lung, and we are going back to the hospital.

She was right so I got admitted to the hospital and placed on blood thinners. I still needed to have the surgery for my back, so they had to figure out how to get the surgery done so that I did not bleed to death. They figured out a way to get it done and I was off from work for six months, thus hitting the brick wall.

I became very depressed and worried how I would be able to care for my family. There were people in my life at the time that made sure that I would be fine. Mr. Harrison the banker, for one, and Mr. James Butler, the other. They both found ways to keep me from financial disaster with a loan and just financial support. I began to question if I could go back to work after being off for a half year. I finally got my pain under control and got off the pain medications that didn't allow me to work.

I returned at a slow pace, and I found that I never missed a beat. Back to doing what I love to do, caring for sick patients in the emergency department.

After returning to work I got offered the director-ship of the department for which I had been the assistant director for many years. I accepted the position and hired several African American doctors to work in the department. They were very competent physicians and well respected by the community.

Our volume grew from 22,000 visits to 32,000 visits. We then decided to renovate the entire emergency department under the leadership of Mr. Jim Nemeth, the COO of the hospital. We were able to raise the money to pay for the project and ran the emergency department without closing our doors. The community was very receptive of the new facility and the staff had more rooms for patient care.

My life took another turn, however. When I saw my doctor, he informed me that my PSA (prostatic surface antigen) was rising, and he had concerns since my father had had prostate cancer.

That is never a good thing to hear.

He referred me to a urologist who recommended a prostate biopsy. I will never forget the day I got the call that my biopsy was positive, and I had prostate cancer. I went to my wife, and she said, We will get through this together. I went to see the oncologist, the cancer doctor, and he gave me several options to consider.

My choice was to have surgery and have it removed. The surgery went well I thought, until I continued to have urinary incontinence while trying to work. I always wondered if I smelled like urine in my clothes. I went back to the urologist, and he recommended a bladder sling to lift my bladder.

That was a disaster, for it made things ten times worse. My depression continued to get increasingly worse, and I turned to my friend and doctor. He referred me to the University of Michigan to a urologist that specializes in urinary incontinence and impotence. He recommended surgery to place implants in my bladder to control the flow of urine.

He also included a treatment for implant for the impedance created by the prostate surgery. My life changed for the better, until my back pain came back with a vengeance. The pain was so bad I could not walk or stand to take a shower. I ended up back in the hospital and needed surgery to place a cage in my back to stabilize the lower vertebrae.

I lost control of my left leg, so I didn't have a choice but to get the surgery. I stayed in the hospital for twenty-eight days to recover and go to rehab to learn how to walk and shower. It took me another three months to recover from this surgery. Again, I was off from work with no pay, worried how I would care for my family.

I was able to borrow from my retirement to keep the household going but it hurt me in the long run for there was less to be able to retire with. After getting the cage my back pain was much better and I regained control of my left leg. I explain all of this because I want people to see that through all the adversity, I have persisted to continue to work, teach and contribute to my community.

My contributions are through my fraternity Kappa Alpha Psi, where I served as the polemarch (president) for two years and led the fraternity to do community service feeding the homeless and several other projects to provide coats and hats for young underprivileged children in the low-income community.

Later I served as the health coordinator for the Northern Province and put on health fairs for the brothers to teach them the importance of health maintenance and having a primary care doctor. We would check blood pressures and explain how high blood pressure is considered the silent killer in the Black community.

It was all such important work!

We talked about diabetes and the complications that come with not being treated and not diagnosed. I quickly learned that there was a fear and mistrust of the healthcare system stemming from the Tuskegee experiment and many other things on social media that were read and found not to be true.

We encouraged them to pick a doctor that you would like as your friend, who will sit and listen to your concerns no matter how big or small they may be. We held a health fair in the local community and my wife noticed a young lady pushing a stroller with a small child.

She approached her and found out she was living in a homeless shelter and didn't have a bed for her child to sleep in. She was just about to move into an apartment but had no furniture. We were able to get her a pack 'n' play. When I delivered it to the new place, she had no furniture. I cried after I left because she was a victim of domestic abuse trying to get back on her feet. I went home and told my wife and we decided to do something about her situation. I reached out to an old friend who had a consignment shop and she agreed to let her come over and pick out her furniture and some clothes to wear and some clothes for her child.

I was touched by the compassion from my friend, and we were able to help someone who was truly in need.

After all these positive things happening in my life, I got a call from my friend Mr. Harrison. He informed me he was having some problems with his memory.

He had been the president of the bank and they decided he needed to retire. He didn't want to retire, so he took the training to become a financial advisor and passed the test. He kept informing me that his job was getting to be more difficult. I encouraged him to go and get tested for dementia.

The results were heartbreaking. We had a heart-to-heart talk and I asked him to retire and travel as much as he could. He was able to visit his daughter who lived in Hawaii whom he had not seen in years. He got a chance to travel to Las Vegas and have fun with family. I watched the progression of his disease to a point where my friend whom I loved didn't recognize me at all anymore and we could not have the wonderful conversations we use to have.

The disease took its toll and ended his life.

I was devastated, and his wife called and asked me to speak at his funeral. She said if anyone could tell the type of person Jack was it would be me, for our friendship was very special to him and he talked about it all the time. I was able to get through the service and spoke of the wonderful times we had playing golf together, eating breakfast in the mornings after I got off from the night shift. He would tell me stories about how the banking system would make differences for people of color, and he hated the culture of racism.

He set out to change that when he helped several of my friends who had businesses and needed financial assistance. He had this saying: IT'S ONLY MONEY, WHAT'S THE PROBLEM?!

Jack will always live in my heart and in my mind,

for he taught so many things about life.

There are some people that you will never forget in your life even after they're gone.

My journey continued, working in the emergency department, and there was a sudden change in the company that had the contract to the emergency department. The communication broke down between the administration of the hospital and the administration of the company.

They both decided to part ways, and the hospital went out and found a new company to come in and take over the hiring and daily functions of the department. I soon realized that I was not a part of this transition.

When I asked if I could continue in my role as medical director the response was absolutely not. Things quickly went sour, and I decided to walk away from thirty-one years of service to this department, which I poured my heart and soul into. What I didn't know at the time was that COVID was coming, and it was the right time for me to step away.

I got a call from my sister that my aunt was in the hospital with abdominal pain, and they could not find a reason for her pain. After several tests they found that she had a condition called ischemic bowel syndrome. The blood supply was cut off to her bowel and they wanted to do surgery.

She refused and I called her and told her that she would die if they did not do the surgery right away. She told me she was ready to go home to be with the Lord. She passed away the next morning.

My heart was broken. I understood why she made her decision, and I had to respect it. She was always an organized person and she left specific instructions on her funeral, cremation, the funeral home to handle the service, and her program for the service.

She prepared us for her death, and she requested that the family all wear white to her funeral.

This was the beginning of many deaths in my family and friendships. I shortly got a call from my friend from medical school that our friend Wiley was in the hospital with liver cancer from Agent Orange when he was in Vietnam in the military. I spoke to him briefly and he passed several days later.

This was very hard for me, for he was the one who

allowed me to stay with him and his family when I had nowhere else to stay in Philadelphia. This was a devastating time for me; I didn't get to attend the funeral, which I had promised in a prior conversation. I then went to my doctor and requested medication for my depression. I had major side effects from the medication, so I had to stop it. The following year after Wiley's passing, I went to visit my mother. She was in great spirits, and I was able to make dinner for her and my sister, and she enjoyed it—the look on her face was priceless.

I didn't know that this would be the last time I would see my mother alive.

I got a call two months after my visit that my mother was admitted to the hospital around the first part of June. She was admitted for what they thought was an infection to her leg.

The infection didn't respond to intravenous antibiotics, and it turns out she had a very rare form of cancer, multiple myeloma, and there were no cures. I would facetime my sister and talk to Mom every day.

She would always be upbeat and tell me she was

going to be okay. The doctors decided to try radiation treatments and they caused her to have severe pain. She became very ill quickly and my next conversation with my sister was about hospice.

I spoke with her via facetime, and she told me she loved me and she wanted to go home. We got her to the house, and she passed away at home like she wanted to. I got home and realized that she too had planned her funeral and paid for the entire funeral, grave, and casket and wrote her own obituary. She wrote out the program for the service and all the people she wanted to play and sing for her funeral.

Her homegoing service was amazing and she planned it all. Her sorority sisters from Alpha Kappa Alpha performed a ceremony and paid tribute to her legacy of sixty-five years of dedicated service to the organization. This was a tremendous loss for me and my sister, for she was the one who took care of mom and my aunt, who were twins. My family was very supportive of me during this difficult time. I soon returned to work and had to push through the loss.

I returned home and went to visit my good friend

and fraternity brother James Butler in the hospital. He was in the hospital six weeks from a heart problem. We talked and I knew at that time he was not doing well. He finally got out of the hospital and two weeks later I got the dreaded call he passed away. I cried and cried for I lost a true friend.

He was there for me for all of my surgeries. We had a group of four of us friends and named ourselves ALL FOUR ONE.

We would meet for dinner once a month at a different restaurant, laugh and talk about everything. This man was a decorated Vietnam veteran with gold and bronze stars for bravery, worked for IBM for thir-ty-three years as a high-level executive and retired. He then entered state government and worked for several governors in the state.

This left a huge void in my heart, and I will always miss him. Just when I thought I was getting a break I got a call that my father was in hospice from his Alz-heimer's disease, and he was not doing well. He passed away six months after my mother. My stepmother took care of him until his death, and she would not let anyone put him in a nursing home. I love and respect her, for she is an angel who came into my dad's life before he got sick, and they had a wonderful life together.

Chapter Five

Loss

Loss is an island every one of us will visit at some point in our lives.

My daughter called my wife to inform her that her grandmother who lived in Philadelphia, my mother-in-law, was having trouble with her memory and her living condition. She had lost a tremendous amount of weight and she was not eating. She was living alone, and the house was in disarray, and she needed to bring her grandmother to live with us, for her grandmother was failing.

We made arraignments to bring her to Michigan. While at the airport my daughter experienced her grandmother pass out in the terminal. She had to go to the emergency room not knowing if she was going to live or die.

It turns out that she was severely dehydrated for the lack of eating and drinking. After IV fluids and hydration she regained her strength and was able to make the trip to live with us in Michigan. When she arrived, we had her evaluated for dementia and the results were devastating.

Her diagnosis was conclusive for the disease, and we were dedicated to caring for her to the end of wherever her disease process would carry her. We were able to find a companion by the name of Rose who accepted her as her mom.

We got the opportunity to see up close and personal what this disease can do to an individual, as she was stripped of her mental faculties, and it progressed to her not being able to communicate.

One morning I went downstairs and found my mother-in-law lying on the floor. She had fallen trying to go to the bathroom. I immediately knew that she had broken her hip.

We called EMS and had her transferred to the emergency department, where her daughter was working. We found out that her hip was broken, and she got admitted for surgery to repair the fracture. We then had to decide to place her in a facility thinking she could rehab and come back home.

This was not the case at all and things started to unravel as she developed an intestinal bleed and we found out that she had a large mass in her colon.

It was felt that the mass was cancer, and we went to her to ask what her wishes would be, and she indicated that she did not want any treatment and to let nature take its course.

We then knew that she would not be able to return to our home. We began to prepare our children and the family for the decision for hospice to alleviate as much suffering as possible. Sometimes loss is sudden and at other times it's a slow burn. My mother-in-law wanted to be buried in her home in Philadelphia and she passed away in our home state of Michigan. We had to plan for her body to be prepared here and make arrangements for her body to be shipped to Philadelphia for her burial. What we didn't know is that we thought she had insurance policies to cover her burial expenses and found out that due to her disease she didn't remember to continue to pay on the policies and they had all lapsed. I mention this because when family members live alone and they have a disease with memory no one has the ability to keep up on the particular things such as insurance payments, etc. We found a way to get her back to Philadelphia and have a wonderful funeral and burial next to her sister.

What grief have you faced?

Losing both my parents within six months was unimaginable but I had to find ways to carry on. I began to see a counselor and saw my doctor to get on some medication to help me deal with the stress and the multiple losses that were so close to my heart. I feel that I am in a better place for I am still working and teaching, touching the lives of young people who desire to become doctors like myself.

One of the most devastating situations I encountered was when I got the call that my friend and best man in my wedding was having difficulty with his memory. I went to visit him on several occasions, and I began to see the decline in his thought process. It got to the point on one visit he no longer recognized me, and he could not care for himself. I thank God for Susan, his life friend and confidante, who cared for him until the end.

Frank never married or had children, but he was the godfather for my oldest daughter. He once told me the closest he had to having children was the kids I had, who he had the opportunity to keep for a week at his home when they were younger. Frank passed away shortly after one of my last visits and he had no family to plan a funeral. We started doing some research to get information on his family and made an obituary and a funeral service. We were not able to attend for we both found out we had COVID prior to leaving for the service. I felt horrible but I knew it was best to keep everyone safe. My daughter was able to attend and speak on our behalf. Frank will always remain in my heart and my mind, for he was a huge part of my success as a doctor today, He left my daughter with a sum of money—I had no idea that he was thinking of her in such an awesome way but I wasn't surprised, for he had a heart of gold.

Some of the accomplishments that I am very proud of are being a father to my wonderful three children, Rhonda, Brittany, and Brandon; being married to the love of my life, my beautiful wife, Beverly; and the four grandchildren, Julius, Jayden, Journey, and Corey; and my son-in-law, Robert. This is my reason for living, for they bring me such joy and happiness in my life after all that I have been through. Other proud moments in this journey of my life were being selected to serve on the Michigan State Medical Board. This appointment is made by the governor of the state of Michigan. I am truly appreciative to Governor Gretchen Whitmer for this opportunity to be able to sit on an awesome board to oversee the doctors in the entire state of osteopathic physicians. I had the opportunity to sit for six years on the board of trustees for the hospital where I work. This was an opportunity to see how the hospital system works and how healthcare was impacted by COVID and the rapid changes in the government's CMS, JCA-HO and insurance companies' impact reimbursement.

This has been an awesome journey for me to live to see sixty-eight years and to live a dream that started with a conversation with my father at the age of five. He wanted to become a doctor and could not make it because of life circumstances but I knew I could dream and make it happen for him. This book is written for all of those individuals who want to dream and make your dreams come true through many ups and downs that will come your way. Let no one ever take your joy and your dreams, for they belong to you.

Chapter Six

Memory

There are some things that are truly unexpected in life and losing your memory or faculties is one of them.

I want to take an opportunity to talk to you about Alzheimer's disease, for it has impacted our lives on multiple occasions with our relatives and very close friends. This is a disease that is very prevalent within the African American community and the difficulty is being able to recognize the symptoms early on and get in to see a doctor for an evaluation and a possible diagnosis.

This is a slow and insidious disease that can be confusing as it progresses to its full-blown potential.

Have you ever walked into a room at home and totally forgot what you went into the room for? Have you walked up to an individual whom you have known before and as soon as you see them you can't remember their name? These are sometimes the subtle signs that the disease is on its way to becoming more prevalent.

So, what should one do when these types of changes start to occur? First and foremost, if you don't have a primary care doctor you must seek out one to care not just for your mind but your overall health. Be up-front and honest with your doctor about your concerns and request that you be tested for the disease, especially if you have a family member who has or had the disease—as in my case, my father and two of his sisters.

Part of my reason for writing this book is to educate and expose you the reader to some of the real-life situations that I have encountered on my journey to live out a dream that started at the age of five years old. I want to get the message out to our young people to make sure their health is a priority early in the teenage years, into the twenties, thirties and on.

We cannot prevent dying, but we sure can prolong life.

The value of this is we must build a foundation for our health for comparison as we age. We often think, I don't need a doctor because I am not sick. I would stop to ask you who taught you to be sick.

This means that you should seek out a doctor and see them at least once a year to get a complete physical exam done with baseline blood work for future reference. Do you think that seeing a doctor one day out of a year is asking too much for your own body and health? I don't think so. Go ahead and make that appointment and ask for what you need for your health.

Health is wealth and prevention is the fire.

Our health is all that we have, for when it fails us it leaves us in a very difficult situation. You are not able to work, make money to pay the bills, or do your daily tasks. So do all of us a favor and advocate for your health by trying to eat right, exercise and avoid the things that are counterproductive to your body.

Chapter Seven

Life

What have I learned on this journey of mine since I have shared so many details of my life?

I've learned a lot and I continue to learn more each day!

One life is short and precious; the life you live is between the dash of sunrise and sunset. What you choose to do in between the dashes is what matters.

It really is true. Make the moment matter.

This is your God-given opportunity to live out your dreams and see them through until it's time to take that one last breath and travel to a land that we on earth have no idea what it will look like. I have learned to love and be compassionate and able to listen to my patients, my family and friends.

I have learned that every day that you wake up is a gift from above and this is the opportunity to make the best of the day, for you never know if this is the day that may be your last, to take that last breath.

That reminds me of a particular situation that my wife and I encountered at a local grocery store. We had just come from a funeral celebration, and she wanted some corn for a meal she wanted to prepare. I said I would stop by the store and get the corn. As I am walking towards the front door of the store, I notice a lady sitting in her car with her feet on the ground leaning over. I went over to see what was wrong and she indicated that she was having difficulty breathing and she had an inhaler in her hand. I noticed she had a friend in the car with her and I told her to call 911 on her phone. As an ER doctor I could tell something was terribly wrong and she became more agitated because of her breathing.

I could hear the sirens in the background, so I knew help was on the way. I tried to get her to use her inhaler, but she quickly became unconscious. By then EMS and the fire department had arrived. I indicated who I was and told them that she was in cardiac arrest. They got her out of the car and laid her down on the pavement. I watched her eyes as she took that last breath. I told my wife I just witnessed someone die in front of my face. To take this a step further I got a call from one of the church members and she indicated that someone told her that a Black doctor was on the scene when this lady who I didn't know had passed away. She wanted to know if me and I said yes, why would you like to know. She told me her daughter lived out of state and she wanted to speak to me. I told her it was fine, and one day I got a call from her daughter.

"Did she die alone?" she asked.

This is a common question in sudden death from loved ones.

"No," I said, reassuring her. "She did not die alone and she did not suffer."

Now I know God is doing His thing for I would never have known the outcome of her death nor talked with her family members unless all that had transpired.

Is it hard being an ER doctor? This is a question I get a lot. Yes, of course it is. But it's a calling for me and I wouldn't change a thing.

Be kind, love, laugh and aways tell the people that you care about that you love them. To our young people, continue to dream big and plan on how you can make your dreams come true.

Sometimes the dashes are very short, and one will not get the opportunity to have a dream, and some will not understand what it is to dream at all. Dreams are the thoughts in our mind that can push us in a direction to accomplish any goals we choose to set for ourselves.

The best advice I can give to you, or anyone is to just go for it. Go for your dreams.

Just believe in yourself and work hard, giving your best in whatever, you choose to do in your life. Once you have given your all there is nothing else to give because it's your best.

What's next?

Dear reader,

Take time to think about the things you want to do

with your life that you have not done. What would you regret at the end of the day? It's never too late to live the life of your dreams, you just must step out on faith. On the pages to follow, take notes about your own life, and the things that you would like to change and the people that you would like to impact. You can do it!

We are all on this journey together. I have dedicated my life to giving my best and I think it's paid off. I want to thank you for reading my story, for I felt it is a story that needed to be told.

During the writing of this book, I found myself pondering life, a lot.

I have thought about some things that may interest you about life itself.

When we are born, we enter into this world through a birth canal from our mothers. When you arrive, the doctors wait for you to take that first breath and cry. This is the beginning of the first dash starting your life, for you to be nurtured and raised to become a productive member of society. We all come through the birth canal with nothing, and all we acquire is through the nurturing process and what we are taught along the way. God planned for us to thrive under some very difficult situations and allow us to grow and learn to become adults. Having parents who care and make sure you are safe during your journey into adulthood has a tremendous impact on your outcome as a teenager and as an adult.

Make time for the people that you love and the ones that love you. Start to dream early—it's okay!—and think about your future and how you will be able to make a contribution to this God-given world that He decided to put you into. I want to remind us all of how precious life is and ask that we find a way to protect our children from being killed on a daily basis in school, on the streets, and sometimes in the home. These are children who will never get to dream or make any contribution to this society. Let's stop the killing, for God cannot be happy with the way that this world is going. Stop and THINK. HE has given us everything we need to live a comfortable life if we choose.

We have clean water, a sun that always shines, and a moon that never goes away. The sky is always blue and the clouds reign above. The rain comes to water the flowers and the crops for our food to eat. He gave us animals for our protein to eat, and clothes to wear on our bodies. So since He has given so much, how about we all make an effort to give back to each other until the end of your dash arrives. The time is now, before you get to take that one breath to take you to the house that the Almighty has prepared for all of us, no matter how young, old or evil.

In conclusion I want to thank Collier media and Dr. Dale Okorodudu who has inspired me to write this book and Tammy Kling for her inspiration and wisdom to help me get this message through. I thank my family, friends, and the patients I have had for the opportunity to care for their lives and be able to save many of them.

When you're writing a book it feels like a legacy, of sorts. There are so many I'd love to thank but most of all I want to thank my wife for her dedication and devotion to our family.

I love you.

....

....

....

....

....

....

....

....

....

....

....

....

....

....

....

....

....Dr Ronald Bishop..

....

....

Dr Ronald Bishop

Dr Ronald Bishop